Penny Copland-Griffiths grew up in Dorset from the age of ten. Inspired by her father's love of history she became involved in amateur archaeology, and was invited to form a project researching the origins of pottery found in the Salisbury by-pass excavation. These finds were traced to East Dorset and thus began twenty-five years of field-work, archaeology, documantary research and oral history. She formed a charitable Trust in 1985 to co-ordinate the work, and is co-author of *Verwood and District Potteries* (1987).

Following page
Potters demonstrating at Cross Roads Pottery, Verwood, in 1926.
Mescheck Sims is throwing on the wheel, Herbert Fry and
Len 'Alfie' Sims are to his left. 'Drummer' Brewer is controlling
the crank that turned the wheel.

DISCOVER DORSET

POTTERY

PENNY COPLAND-GRIFFITHS

THE DOVECOTE PRESS

A posy dish made by the Cross Roads Pottery,
Verwood, probably in the 1920's or 30's.

First published in 1998 by The Dovecote Press Ltd
Stanbridge, Wimborne, Dorset BH21 4JD

ISBN 1 874336 57 1

Series designed by Humphrey Stone

Typeset in Sabon by The Typesetting Bureau
Wimborne, Dorset
Printed and bound by Baskerville Press, Salisbury, Wiltshire

A CIP catalogue record for this book is available
from the British Library

CONTENTS

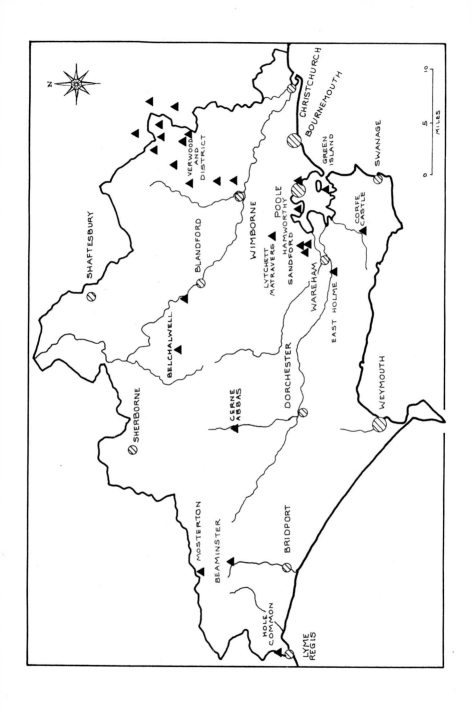

INTRODUCTION

Throughout much of Dorset's history pottery has been an important and thriving industry. Geologically the county varies from the chalk downlands, and the limestones of Purbeck and Portland, to the poorer soils of the heathland (famous for its connections with Thomas Hardy and his renowned Egdon Heath) and the multicoloured clays of the Reading and London beds which stretch from north to south in the eastern part of the county.

From Neolithic times (5,000 years ago) man has utilised the same clay beds for making pottery, creating various methods by which to produce his wares. Bonfire, or open firing, is a means of firing pottery in a temporary, open construction in which the vessels are laid on a bed of fuel and covered by more fuel. The pots are ready when the fuel has burnt itself out. Clamp or pit kilns are a development between open firing and kiln firing, when the vessels were stacked together with the fuel in a shallow pit covered with more fuel topped by a temporary covering such as stones or turfs. Kiln firing is a means of firing pottery in a closed construction consisting of a firebox and a chamber in which the vessels are separated from the fuel. In medieval times it was composed of clay and by post medieval times of brick. The kiln enables the potter to control the admission of air, when free admission of air (oxygen) leads to the production of orange to red throughout the body of the pot and when excluding air (oxygen) results in grey to black pots or surfaces.

As more substantial materials were used in the construction of later medieval and post medieval kilns, remains of the industry and associated buildings from this period are more readily found,

A map showing some present day and known historic areas of pottery making in Dorset. Keysworth and Sibley are next to Sandford.

enabling archaeologists to identify the extent of pottery works of the last four hundred years. Apart from specialised pieces produced for weddings or special events, which were usually dated or decorated and have survived in museums and private collections, the examination of pit groups from various excavations around the county have helped to identify products from various sites.

On the heaths of south and east Dorset medieval potters found the land they required. Gradually the industry dominated areas of Dorset clustered around the edge of the clay beds, where there was also a plentiful supply of the other materials they needed: sand, water and easily accessible fuel. They fired their kilns with the peaty turf and furze of the heathland and with the abundant timber from an area which fringed the New Forest.

This situation is typical wherever the necessary clay beds are present. However, it is not often that remains of an industry survive so well. In Dorset this is due to the fact that some of the land where it flourished is still in the hands of private estates, and therefore has proved less vulnerable to the building programmes which have hit so many parts of Britain this century.

The kilns in Dorset only produced earthenware, the commonest form of pottery until the mid-nineteenth century. In the east of the county forty known sites have been identified, and although the odd pottery kiln has been identified in other parts of the county, the pottery from the area seems to have been an important centre for the industry. It is known as Verwood Ware because the last working pottery closed in 1952 in the village of Verwood. Wares like tin glaze, porcelain or stone-ware were not made in the county. Fine ware production only started in the late nineteenth century in Poole and 'craft' wares in the twentieth century.

These earthenwares known as country pottery or coarse ware, provided utensils for all necessary domestic requirements. In medieval times the jug, bowl and cooking pot were the main types that the potter produced, but by the end of the sixteenth century an extremely wide range of wares was being produced.

Most of the earthenware pots were glazed. This was achieved by various methods, but common to all was the procedure of covering the ware with a chemical coating, which, when exposed to heat,

A 'waster' lead glazed chafing dish from the excavation of a seventeenth century kiln in the village of Horton. It was used with hot charcoal in the bowl to warm food at the table or for simple cooking.

resulted in a hard surface. Depending on the use of the pot, so glaze was applied for decorative purposes or to make the pot waterproof. A lead glaze was achieved by applying powdered lead oxide (litharge) or galena (lead sulphate). In medieval times other substances would be added to a lead glaze to produce different colours such as copper filings to produce a brilliant green. The addition of iron would give a range of golden browns and yellows depending on the amount of iron added. In the village of Horton in East Dorset the remains of kilns with heaps of sherds from failed pots have been found. On examining the glaze it has been revealed that the clay itself contained iron, leaving a distinctive iron flecking which helps to identify pottery from this site when examining excavated pit groups. Manganese was also often added, resulting in a rich dark brown glaze. Several hamlets in East Dorset made fine examples of this brown ware.

Poole Pottery's East Quay works in about 1914 showing the procedure for making floor tiles. The tiles are about to be dipped into glaze before the final firing.

Although no medieval sites have been positively located, certain areas in east and west Dorset where limited excavation and research have taken place indicate possible early potting.

Much more information has been revealed about the industry in post medieval times, particularly in the east of the county. More importantly, because the last working pottery closed as late as 1952, reminiscences of some of the last workers have provided a unique insight into a way of life that is now extinct.

Fine ware was beginning to be made in Poole following an explosion of activity in the late nineteenth century. This evolved from a firm started by Jesse Carter and now known as the well-established Poole Pottery. Initially the business in Poole manufactured tiles, but with family involvement became more widely diversified into lustre-glazed pieces, terracotta garden ware, majolica and various other forms of pottery, as popular demand requested decorative as well as useful ware.

A covered jar with a pale ash glaze made by Richard Batterham.

During the twentieth century the craft potteries began to develop, Sibley and Keysworth near Wareham being some of the first and most well known. Over the last fifty years the emphasis has changed from larger industrial units towards individuals working as studio potters. Here it is much more difficult to be selective, because the number of studio potters working in the county constantly fluctuates. For the purposes of this book I have mentioned only a handful of the potters who now live and work in Dorset, but Richard Batterham and Carol Lodder (north Dorset), the Eales family and Paul Green (west Dorset), and Adrian Lewis-Evans, Jonathan Garratt, and Matt-Hew Davies (east Dorset) do reflect the variety of styles and wares that make contemporary ceramics so fascinating.

VILLAGES AND HAMLETS OF EAST DORSET

Travelling from Fordingbridge to Wimborne you still pass through many hamlets where small traditionally-farmed field systems have at first glance appeared to shape the history of the area. Such is the character of the landscape you would be forgiven for failing to realise that in recent centuries it formed the backdrop to one of Dorset's most significant cottage industries, for only within the last twenty-five years has research shown that pottery making was vital to the economy of the region.

ALDERHOLT

An extract from a letter written in 1854 by William Key of Alderholt to Lord Salisbury (the Lord of the Manor) tells us how vital were the village's potteries, and how many people depended on them for a living. The £8 cost of a licence to sell their wares by horse and wagon was crippling and the fine for failing to have such a licence far worse. Thus Key's letter is a plea for the very existence of his community:

> The sum for a licence is equal I believe to the Staffordshire ware of which the potters say a man can take a load worth £20 with one horse, but that £3 is the average value of a load of our ware. I have been soundly informed that three kilns, Zebedee's and Thornes at Crindall and Baileys at Alderholt (Mowlands the second at Alderholt has just been shut up), support almost entirely one hundred and twenty three men, women and children, independent of the employment it gives to the wood and turf cutters, many of whom are unfit for farm labouring, and must get a living.

Alderholt, which was once part of the parish of Cranborne and detached late last century, has now become quite a large scattered

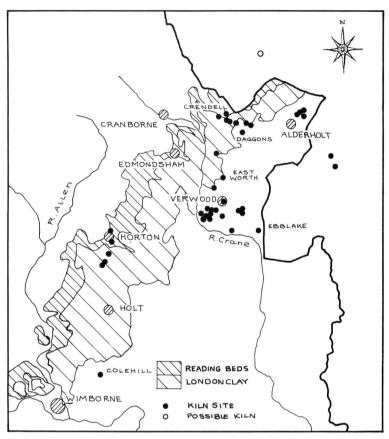

Map showing extent of the known post-medieval pottery sites in Dorset and the clay beds.

village, but remains of the potting community can still be found. One kiln mound survives. Another was partially destroyed in the 1950's by having a bungalow built on its foundations. Several other sites can be identified by their scatters of wasters.

Many families were involved in potting from the thirteenth century and names such as Atwater, Major, Henning, Francis, Shearing, Viney and Bailey can still be found in the telephone directory today. One can still talk to descendants of this potting community.

COLEHILL

Colehill is now a suburb of Wimborne, but documents tell us that once it was involved in pot making. Little is known of the extent of the industry here and with only one eighteenth to nineteenth century site identified (long since destroyed) a lot more research is needed. Wimborne Minster's church wardens' accounts from the fourteenth century show that pots were purchased for acoustic purposes to help amplify the voice of the priest. The church in Tarrant Rushton still has two earthenware acoustic pots set into the wall of the chancel arch. Medieval potters would have been commissioned to make these, probably from somewhere in the locality.

CRENDALL

A map of 1608 shows the extent of clay pits and the size of the potting community in Crendall (the old name for "clay ground"). Scatters of sherds can be found in ditches and fields. The Zebedee family, involved in potting from before church records began, still farm here. A dutch barn has been erected on one of the sites but careful examination of the surrounding area confirms its location. Another site, excavated by Salisbury Museum Research Group in 1975, was run by the Vincent family between 1770 and 1810. Members of the Kibby, Harvey, Fry, Chubb, Shearing and Thorn families worked other sites. Today Crendall is just a little group of scattered cottages, but areas where clay was dug can still be seen.

DAGGONS

The hamlet of Daggons now only consists of two or three cottages. Its potteries were probably established in the eighteenth century and four sites can be identified by sherd scatters. Two of these are represented by large amounts of wasters in the gardens, verified when bungalows were being built. The Sims, Bailey, Hellior, Zebedee, West and Foster families were involved in these potteries and many of their descendants still live in and around Daggons today.

DAMERHAM

This is still quite a substantial village but little is yet known other than a documentary reference for medieval potting in the thirteenth century. No kiln site has been precisely located although field names do give clues to past involvement, such as Crockers Copse.

EASTWORTH

The hamlet of Eastworth has all but disappeared, yet it is known that three potteries flourished here in the seventeenth century. Two sites have been found but sadly one of these was destroyed as recently as the 1970's. Records show that potters involved were from the Sims, Foreman, Gibbs, Doe, Williams and Henning families.

EDMONDSHAM

Today Edmondsham is quite a large village. Only one site has been located and dated as approximately eighteenth century. It is possible that more sites await discovery and documentary evidence hints that there is more than one site. Records show that two families by the names of Lawrence and Kerley were involved in potting.

HARBRIDGE

The village of Harbridge could scarcely even be called a hamlet now. Passing through you may come across a small scattering of thatched cottages, but no real centre to what used to be a thriving community. It is known that two potteries flourished here in the eighteenth century, being worked amongst others by the families of Sutton, Hart, Downs, Whitfield, Hall and Shearing. No visible remains survive, though scatters of wasters can be found beneath the meadow grass or the surface of fields after ploughing.

The village of Horton is still a substantial one. Within the parish lie five kiln sites, although three are closer to the modern town of Verwood. The two kilns found in and around the village were identified by their extensive sherd scatter and are seventeenth century. The best known pottery site, due to various excavations which have taken place in the late 1980's and early 1990's, lies in the heart of the village. Documentary records show that there were two potters in this area. It is clear from the Court Books that the major clay source was on Haythorne Common and there is evidence of two potters exploiting it. William Frost was working by 1616 when he appeared in the Court for digging clay in the 'Lord's waste'. Further presentments for similar offences occur in later years and the business appears to have ceased following his death in 1659. His son William appears to be potting but whether he took over his father's kiln is not yet known. The Court Book refers to him clay digging at Haythorne in 1684.

Elias Talbot was working from at least 1652 when, on the first of many occasions, he was fined for digging clay in Haythorne, 'having no right to dig there'. He was granted copyhold on a cottage and a plot of land on Charlbury Common, just beyond the Horton boundary. In his will of 1672, he is stated to be of Horton, but property in both Horton and Chalbury is mentioned. His copyhold passed to his wife, but the kiln was taken over jointly by his wife and Richard Lacy, his brother-in-law. Within a few years Thomas Lacy, presumably Richard's son, was running it and continued to do so until his death in 1711, when the business appears to have ceased.

Excavations at the pottery unearthed some excellent examples of different vessels that were in production. In some instances, it was possible to reassemble their complete forms. Some, because of the shape of the pot, actually remained intact but with sufficient damage to be termed by the potter as unfit for sale. Types such as delicate saucers and ring-necked jugs showed that the maker was influenced by imported wares. Others included mugs, pipkins, (a saucepan with legs), along with ridge tiles and bread ovens.

Above A 'waster' lead glazed ring-necked jug from the excavation of a seventeenth century kiln in the village of Horton. 'Wasters' were cracked or damaged pots not fit for sale, but because many were discarded at the kiln site a number have survived.

Opposite page A 'waster' lead glazed costrel, also known as a Dorset 'owl', from a seventeenth century kiln in Horton. They were often used by farmworkers for carrying cider or beer.

The other site, five minutes walk from the centre, lies in pasture, and features can still be seen, such as the outline of brick kilns and the scattering of pottery sherds. Richard Harding's map of 1640 confirms that William Frost occupied this area, and it is possible that they were the potters at the excavated site – especially as samples of pottery from the unexcavated site are very similar in form and glaze from the excavated site.

An eighteenth century bushel pan inserted into the cob wall of one of the buildings at Cracked Pot cottage. Its purpose is unknown.

Of the three kilns situated nearer to the town of Verwood, two have disappeared and one has been scheduled as an ancient monument. The monument now known as Cracked Pot Cottage is a fine example of an eighteenth century pottery with kiln mound, drying shed, apprentice's cottage and a cob cottage which has been updated and extended. One notable feature is a pot set into the wall of what was probably once an outhouse. No one has yet been able to explain this feature, which is also found in other East Dorset pottery communities. This site was run by the Henning family, who seem to have moved from Alderholt in 1730 to set up business. After his death Robert Henning's son Richard took over. The latter was followed by another Richard, possibly a grandson, who seems to have ended the business in about 1840. The other pottery was not far from the Hennings. We know it was run by the Ferrett family in the 1840's, but a bungalow was built on the site in the 1960s and little remains except scatters of sherds in the garden.

Holt is a large scattered village and several pottery sites lie on the edge of Holt in an area called Holt Forest. Three can be identified by their sherd scatters. It appears that brick and tile production also took place on these sites, as in Horton. It is known that the Frampton family were involved, whose descendants today run a well-known local building company.

A map showing these villages reveals gaping holes where, as yet, no indications of the industry have been found. The inaccessibility of the land or a lack of documentary clues are just two of the obstacles that thwart the search for further evidence of this once flourishing industry. But it seems certain that more sites will finally be found, and that the full story of pottery making in the smaller hamlets of East Dorset has yet to be told.

VERWOOD

Verwood was the most important centre in the later history of the East Dorset pottery industry: indeed it has given its name to all the wares associated with the area. The last pottery, situated in the centre of town, only closed in 1952. Documentary and photographic records survive in abundance. There are rich verbal recollections and a number of structures still survive.

Verwood was originally a scattered hamlet that developed around the pottery industry. The potters encroached upon the common land because the Enclosure Acts of the eighteenth and nineteenth centuries in more fertile lands had prevented the erection of more kilns. Verwood's present population of more than 12,000 is a far cry from its humble beginnings. It has never been a typical Dorset village clustered around a church. In the late nineteenth century it separated from its mother parish of Cranborne, creating its own parish and church, and land was sold off at different stages by the Salisbury, Shaftesbury and Normanton Estates. When the pottery industry died the surrounding area was so poor agriculturally that developers moved in and began to buy the land. The profile of

Cross Roads Pottery, Verwood, in the 1930's.

Verwood was to change so radically that never again would this East Dorset back-water be the quiet little hamlet it once was. It is now a sprawling overspill town complete with shopping centres and industrial parks – even a mayor.

Happily however there are still many descendants of potting families living in and around the town. Names such as Andrews, Bailey, Brewer, Budden, Dewey, Ferrett, Foreman, Fry, Hurle, King, Lockyer, Rook, Shearing, Sims and Thorn, often date back to ancestors who were involved in the industry. By adapting to Verwood's changing fortunes, both the Sims and Shearing families have become successful and well-known building firms.

The earliest known pottery site in Verwood is possibly very late seventeenth century. It lies in an area called Ebblake, on the eastern edge of Verwood, where the remains of a kiln have recently been uncovered. Another likely early site is in Potterne, an area south of the town centre. Scant documentary evidence has been found, but the spread of sherds shows that the pottery is probably eighteenth century. It lies in pasture and other features, such as building platforms, can be seen there. Place-name references for as early as 1280 are known for Potterne Farm, which interpreted from the Old English *Pott* and *Earn* means 'Building where pots are made, a pottery.'

Of the eleven known sites in Verwood, the most famous and best documented of all is the Cross Roads Pottery, which first started in

Cross Roads pottery in 1926 with potter Herbert Bailey demonstrating to visitors.

[23]

A twentieth century pitcher, probably made at the Cross Roads Pottery,
which has been decorated at a later date by the owner.

the early the nineteenth century and whose centenary was celebrated
in a newspaper article of 1912. The Tithe Map of 1847 shows that
Robert Shearing was then tenant, but in the latter part of the century
a relative called Mr Ferrett was in charge. By the turn of the century
Fred Fry was running the pottery. Fred was a respected and popular
Verwood figure and many people remember him well. He employed
a team including 'Drummer' George Brewer, Len Sims, Jim Scammel,
Harold Churchill and Herbert Bailey – all of whom can be identified

in old photographs and recalled in memory. In spite of Fred Fry's innovative and valiant efforts the potteries were already declining fast. He received commissions from people like the famous archaeologist, General Pitt-Rivers, who ordered reproduction Greek and Roman pots as presents for his friends. Fred also produced new forms of decorated and rustic pottery, perfumed bricks and vessels for lavender water in an attempt to diversify. But the changes were in vain. Mass-produced pottery from the Midlands and tin and

An early nineteenth century costrel. Incised into the buff clay is the name Oba Sims, the person for whom it was probably made. Four pierced lugs for leather thongs hang at the shoulders.

Above Potters unloading the kiln at the Cross Roads Pottery in the 1930s.
From left to right: Jim Scammel, Drummer Brewer, Len Sims,
Mesheck Sims and Bert Bailey.
Opposite page Herbert Fry applying handles on vases and jugs at
the Cross Roads Pottery in 1926.

enamel wares were rapidly gaining popularity and replacing everyday earthenware.

Fred Fry sold the Cross Roads Pottery in 1925 to Robert Thorn. Work ceased for a time but was restarted by Robert's son Horace two years later, under the management of Mesheck Sims, who together with his team of assistants continued the struggle to make the pottery profitable. A woman, Gertie Gilham from Poole Pottery, worked at the Cross Roads in the late forties and early fifties and tried to introduce more modern and efficient potting methods. So traditional were the resident potters that new ways seemed too foreign and were ignored. Herbert Bailey, who had been Mesheck Sims' assistant, took over the pottery for the last decade of its working life. He and his assistant Len Sims continued faithfully to the end. Tragically, nothing survives of a business that in its heyday was the most important and best recorded

of all East Dorset's potteries. Both the large and small kilns were destroyed in the sixties when a bungalow was built on them. All that remains is one drying shed.

It has often been suggested that the Cross Roads pottery's future might well have been secured if it could have held on for a further ten or twenty years. New trends in consumer tastes encouraged the re-establishment of smaller more personal craft industries as people increasingly became disenchanted with mass produced wares. In spite of the interest of Britain's most influential contemporary craft potter, Bernard Leach, the Cross Roads pottery finally closed in 1952.

Of the other potteries in Verwood, three nineteenth century sites were in an area known as Black Hills on the eastern side of the town. Sadly little remains today except a cottage known as Olde Farmhouse, once part of the Sims' pottery, and the road name, Sherd Close. The other two sites were run by the Bailey and Sims families.

At the same time as the last of these three sites was being destroyed, a Charitable Trust was registered to research and record the remains of the industry. The emergency measures that had to be taken to salvage a sample from this site gave the final impetus to the creation of the Verwood and District Potteries Trust in 1985, by which time Verwood's massive development boom was well underway. Whilst field work was being undertaken near the Black Hills sites, a rather dilapidated little cob cottage was noticed. It was due to be pulled down as part of a building programme. On closer inspection it was found that four pots had been inserted into the inside of the cob walls. Permission was granted by the developer for the pots to be carved out of the walls before the building was demolished and these are now in the Salisbury and South Wiltshire Museum. This cob building had been part of the Sims pottery and further pots can be seen inserted in the walls of the Olde Farmhouse.

Near the Monmouth Ash public house is another site, probably started in the 1840's by the Bailey family and continued by the Sims' family. The late Miss Gerty Sims could recall her father potting there and spoke of the gradual diversification of her father's business into the building trade as his pottery work interests began to waver and die. By the early 1900's the process was complete and Freddy Sims had become a full time builder.

A small nineteenth century costrel for holding lavender water or perfume. Incised on the base is the name of the perfumerer, Rivers & Hill Company, Broadstone, and inscribed is a record of its purchase from the Cross Roads Pottery, Verwood.

On Dewlands Common there remains a remarkably complete nineteenth century site, which had been run by the Andrews family. In the 1980's it was scheduled as an ancient monument and was later bought by a sympathetic builder, Tony Pharoah. Although it has subsequently changed hands, the kiln mound, a large drying shed, a partial shed leading to the kiln and a small cob building survive. Three other eighteenth/nineteenth century sites which lie on the fringe of Dewlands Common were destroyed and now lie under recently built houses. The odd scatter of pottery sherds can be found in ditches and gardens and a few structures that may have been pottery buildings have been incorporated into new housing, but little else remains of these sites.

Pottery making in Dorset was by no means confined to the east and the south of the county and a number of potteries existed elsewhere. The full extent of Dorset's potting history is still not known, for example the origins of a distinctively decorated earthenware commonly found excavated in Dorchester still remain unclear.

In West Dorset, in Beaminster, Stevenson in 1815 lists 'two potteries for coarse ware'. It is known that in the seventeenth century a family called Hearn were involved in potting, followed by the Chick family. In the nineteenth century, Abraham Meech, Robert Chambers, Robert and George Hallett were recorded as owners of a pottery in Hogshill Street, but by 1897 permission for the Grammar School to be built on this premises had been given, so clearly the industry had closed down. Certain indications hint that the poor quality of the clay produced poor quality pots, and this could have been one of the reasons for the decline of the business.

East Holme in the Isle of Purbeck has quite substantial records of the Dover family potting here in the seventeenth and eighteenth centuries. Field names such as Potter's Field survive, as do quantities of waster sherds indicating that pottery making had taken place in the area. It is quite like Verwood (East Dorset) pottery, but the body tends to be greyer and the glaze thicker and wetter looking, however similarities in pottery forms can be seen.

On Hole Common large amounts of eighteenth century wasters have been found on a site near to the Penn Inn in the far north end of Lyme Regis parish. The pottery has more in common with Devon kilns than Verwood. The mid-eighteenth century kiln discovered produced a wide range of forms including jugs, dishes and bowls, most of which were slip decorated. Trailed slip and sgraffito patterns were used and some vessels had incised inscriptions. Documentary references show records for the marriages of two potters called John Mitchell in 1742 and a Joshua Case in 1762. It is possible these are connected with the pottery.

MAKING AND SELLING

With so many different sources to draw information from it is possible to gain a vivid and accurate account of traditional methods of pottery making and selling which remained the same over many hundreds of years. Dorset potters were conservative by nature and remained largely unaffected by the industrialisation of the nineteenth and twentieth centuries. They continued to use the same methods as those used by the Alderholt and Horton potters of the seventeenth century. Nearly all the family members were involved in helping to sustain the pottery in one way or another, whether it was collecting timber for firing the kiln, digging clay, helping prepare the pots or selling them.

CLAY DIGGING

The clay was cut out in blocks with a short, two-handled, narrow-bladed spade. Throughout the seventeenth and eighteenth century there are many references in Manor Court Rolls to the failure of potters to re-fill their clay-pits, which became a constant source of danger to travellers and grazing animals.

The orders of the Manor Court seem to have been frequently disregarded. The problem was apparently solved by the Lord of the Manor requiring each potter to take out a bond guaranteeing his good behaviour on pain of a forfeiture of £10. One of these records the 'Bond of Nicholas Francis of Alderholt in the parish of Cranborne potter in £10 to the Earl of Salisbury, 25th March 8 George II, 1735'. It goes on to grant Francis a licence to 'dig and raise clay for his own use by proper workman appointed by the Earl, upon the Earl's waste land called Crendell Common, in the manor, for seven shillings, yearly rent five shillings. The condition of this obligation is that Francis shall employ workman for the above purpose and pay the above rent and shall fill up and level all such pits as shall be opened for digging and raising clay, and shall contribute his share of charges towards repairing the King's highway between Crendall Gate and an oak called Gold Oak on that common, leading from Cranborne to Fordingbridge. Also that he shall not cut or cause to be cut any turf, heath or furze or bushes on the said waste land, to be burnt or employed by him on his kiln or otherwise for his carrying on of the trade of a potter, to the injury of the said Earl or his tenants in their rights in the said common or waste land.'

Although there are earlier documentary references, it is clear that from about 1500 to 1742 adequate supplies were being obtained from the common at Crendell and after that deposits were exhausted. During the eighteenth and nineteenth centuries the western side of Crendell was exploited in fields that still bear names such as Clay Grounds and Old Clay Grounds. By the twentieth century small quantities of clay were being dug at Verwood and Corfe Mullen, usually for mixing with that from Holwell, which had now become a major source. Nevertheless problems still threatened the livelihood of the community, as a letter of 1909 from Fred Fry, owner of the Cross Roads Pottery in Verwood, shows only too clearly:

We regret the Bell Trustees have decided to stop the clay digging – you are aware that the pottery working is practically the sole industry of Verwood (excepting brick making), and many poor people depend on their living by the industry. On behalf of three other potters and myself, we shall be very pleased if you would represent our case to Lord Salisbury as a means of taking some land to enable you to supply us as heretofore. We would give you the usual undertaking to remove the top soil, and level down to the utmost of our ability. Giving to depth and wet season we have only dug 40 yards ie 40 ton for the four potteries. Firewood is also brought from Lord Salisbury through George Fry of Crindall.
Following is a list of people engaged.

Potters	8
Labourers	10
Hawkers carrying brooms & pottery local made	12
	30

A still from the unique five minute film made in 1917 by Charles Urban
about the Cross Roads Pottery. The film was found in 1989 when a cinema in
Derbyshire closed down, and is now housed in the National Film Archive.
The still shows clay being treaded to remove any stones and improve its
consistency. The boy on the right is Len 'Alfie' Sims, the boy
on the left is unknown.

CLAY PREPARATION

When the clay arrived at the pottery it was mixed with water in a pit
and left to soak for several days, helping to reduce the clay to a
plastic state. It was then shovelled onto a brick floor sprinkled with
sand and then wedged (a method by which a man trampled the clay
by foot supporting himself with a stout stave of wood). One of the
workers, Len Sims, used to liken the process to a 'lady making pastry.

Left to right: 'Drummer' Brewer and Len Sims preparing clay in 1926 at Cross Roads Pottery, Verwood.

You trod it, rolled it up and trod it out again'. And Len should know, because for 35 years up to 1952 this was one of his jobs at Cross Roads pottery. The worked clay would finally be hand wedged and weighed, ready for the 'master potter' to throw.

MAKING POTS

Nearly all the pottery was wheel thrown, with the exception of dripping pans and saucers in the seventeenth and eighteenth centuries and ridge tiles which were moulded. Evidence of wheel throwing is shown in the will of Elias Talbot of Horton in 1672 when he leaves to his kinsman Richard Lacy 'the boards, wheel and the use of the shop and kiln after my decease.' Photographs from this century show that the potters adapted the wheels to be operated by an assistant. An apprentice sat beside the wheel pushing and pulling a pole attached to a crank, thus providing the constant motion needed by the potter. There were two wheels at the Cross Roads Pottery, the one crank driven and another more mechanically advanced, hand

Mesheck Sims throwing pots inside a mud building at the Cross Roads Pottery, Verwood, in the 1930's. The apprentice is operating the crank that turned the wheel.

operated with bicycle pedals, a chain and cogs. The pots were thrown directly on the wheel head and were detached by slicing off with wire. It is said that a potter would throw as much as forty to fifty pounds of clay to produce a bushel pan, which were a popular line, used not only for its measure but also for storing water when households did not have piped water.

Most pots of all periods were undecorated, except for use of simple incised wavy or straight lines. Rouletting and finger-impressed bands were applied whilst the pots were on the wheel. Examples from the seventeenth century kiln site of Horton show such lines (a comb being an old method of producing these) and finger impressions. In

A pitcher (jug) being thrown on a wheel by Fred Fry. Note the posy bowl and other vessels in the background.

the eighteenth century rouletting was developed. A cogged wheel, perhaps from an old clock, was mounted in a handle to produce a device like a pastry wheel which was held against the side of the pot whilst it was still rotating. Many different designs could be produced using this method. From the later 19th century incised decoration was sometimes added, often with the name of the recipient but rarely with the name of the maker. It is said that the pottery would have demonstration days when visitors would be encouraged to put their names on pots, the potter would then fire them and visitors would then be allowed to take them home.

In the late nineteenth and early twentieth century 'rustic' ware became fashionable – such as garden pots resembling sections of tree trunks. The irregularities of the bark and even the appearance of knots were effected by combing the surface of the thrown clay. Pots from the very last years of the industry reveal the use of a stamp, the name Verwood impressed on the base of the vessel.

Once thrown the pots were dried, outside in summer or inside in winter. Blackened roof timbers in the one surviving building at the Cross Roads Pottery bear witness to the practice of drying pots inside with heath and turf fires. It was essential that the pots were completely dry otherwise an explosion could take place in the kiln destroying not only the damp pot but others around it. A record from 1758 shows that the potters could be fined a penalty of £2 if they were caught cutting furze, heath or turf for burning in the drying houses or kilns, if they were not commoners with the rights to cut fuel.

A still from the 1917 film showing pottery being placed by the potter and a boy apprentice to dry on boards before being fired.

GLAZING

The pottery was lead glazed. Elias Talbot's will of 1672 bequeaths to his son-in-law, Richard Lacy, 'all my lead in the house and a pot to melt lead in'. The pot was covered or dipped in urine, sprinkled with the prepared litharge (molton lead mixed with barley meal), dried still further and then fired. When the dangers of lead became apparent an Act of Parliament was passed after the First World War which prohibited the further use of litharge. It was replaced by a commercially produced galena from Leeds which was mixed with water and applied with a brush.

In earlier days vessels were more likely to be glazed inside and out, but latterly the potters became more mean with their glaze, probably due to the price, and only slimmer vessels were glazed all over. Various colours were produced, ranging from an apple green to oranges and yellows. The final colour depended on the position of the pot in the kiln, impurities in the lead, minerals in the clay and on the firing conditions. In the seventeenth century a few forms were given a glaze with copper filings in to produce an emerald green colour. In the eighteenth century manganese was added to the glaze, producing a rich dark chocolate brown. Samples of this have been found on sites in the hamlets of Crendell and Daggons and in the recently excavated site in Ebblake on the edge of Verwood. (Often sold through the markets of Salisbury, these dark pots were erroneously classed as 'Wiltshire Brown Ware' by late nineteenth century collectors).

THE KILN

From the seventeenth century most of the kilns were free-standing open-topped brick cylinders, up to ten feet or so in diameter and of similar height. The kiln would be surrounded by a mound of clay, soil and broken pottery. This mound provided both insulation and support for the structure. Firing was effected through a single stoke pit outside the mound, connected by a flue leading to the furnace chamber at the base of the cylindrical oven. A series of brick arches

A still from the 1917 film showing the kiln being loaded prior to firing.

above the furnace chamber supported a perforated floor on which the pottery was stacked. The flattened top of the kiln mound served as a working area for loading and unloading. One mound at Verwood still has a small adjacent building which provided shelter for the potter or fireman during the early stages of firing, when constant attention was essential.

One exception to the usual structure comes from the Horton kiln excavation, which showed that later in the life of the kiln a second flue was opened at its west end. Another is the recently excavated Ebblake kiln, which appears to have been built into a bank, rather than having a mound built around it, and the kiln appears to be square rather than round.

STACKING

One of the problems encountered by potters when they stack glazed ware in a kiln is the running of the glaze during firing and the consequent adhesions of neighbouring pots when the fired kiln has cooled. They usually overcame this by placing old pottery sherds between the wares, in some cases manufacturing specialised shapes to separate their pots. Sometimes saggars were used; these were containers, made of clay, in which smaller pots were packed in the kiln to protect them from harmful flames and from sticking together.

In the seventeenth century Horton kiln no kiln furniture was found in the excavation. However the excavation of Crendall's eighteenth century kiln revealed a few pieces of kiln furniture in the form of wedges and ring props.

In the nineteenth and twentieth centuries once stacking was completed up to the top of the oven, large flat sherds were placed across the load, followed by smaller pieces above these to act as a heat baffle and to provide an insulated layer through which smoke and hot gases could escape.

The kiln was loaded from above. The pots were carried on to the platform or flat area at the top of the kiln and then handed down into the oven. They were positioned by the potter himself to ensure stability and an even distribution of heat. Gertie Sims, the daughter of potter Freddy Sims of Verwood, recalled the disastrous aftermath of a kiln collapse and her mother's tearful cries that they would have no food for many weeks to come. It was important that the pots were carefully positioned to ensure stability and an even distribution of heat. Little kiln furniture was used in the stacking of pots and each was carefully placed to support not only its neighbour but those above as well.

At the Cross Roads pottery the man doing the stacking actually stood on the unfired pots, his weight being spread by the use of boards to fit the base of bushel pans. Sometimes fired pots were included to strengthen the stack. Nests of up to six pans were arranged in an inverted position on the oven floor and successive layers were staggered so that each pot rested across two or three vessels in the layer below. When necessary, sherds were inserted to

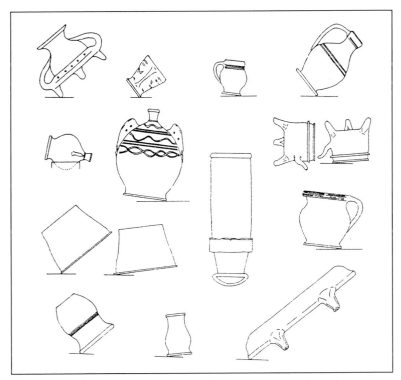

Pots from the seventeenth century kiln at Horton shows how they were placed for firing, indicated by the run of the glaze.

Master potter Fred Fry stoking the kiln, a remarkable still from the 1917 film.

prevent glazed vessels from sticking together. Small pots were fitted into gaps between larger ones. In the last days of the industry rings were used to separate pots, and it is known that Gerty Gilham, from Poole Pottery did try unsuccessfully to use saggers. Essentially the Cross Roads pottery used very little kiln furniture.

All the pots were fired once only, baking the ware and fluxing the glaze in the same operation. The kilns were wood-fired. Early inventories suggest that it was not unusual for a potter to possess wood and faggots to the value of at least £20, a thousand faggots costing about £2 at this time. The source of much of the fuel is indicated by numerous references in the Cranborne Manor Court Rolls to the unlicensed activities of potters. A 1664 example tells how several potters of Alderholt were summoned to the court for cutting turf in the common and common wastes. In 1709 Richard Harvey was presented for 'cutting a great number of Heath faggots . . . to burn his pots . . . to the great distruction of the common.' Local turfs were said to have been the roots of heather from which the soil had been shaken out. Firings took place approximately every seven weeks.

In the last years of the industry the potters purchased loppings from trees felled in the district. Pine was the most sought after, but in the final years there was a great shortage of timber and the potters made use of any wood available.

The fire was started in the mouth of the flue with small sticks, the temperature gradually being increased over three or four days as larger branches and split logs were fed in. The hot gases passed into the furnace chamber, through the perforated floor into the oven and thence up to the stacked pottery. During the last day the faggots were used in 'burning off', the intention being to produce a final burst of intense heat to 'flash the glaze', during which flames emerged several feet out of the top of the kiln. It is said that around a ton of wood was used with each firing.

Temperatures (which seemed not to exceed about 1,000 centigrade) were judged by eye. Some potters would watch particular bricks in the kiln structure until they glowed at the correct red heat. Sometimes a small pot was placed so that it could be removed from the kiln during firing for inspection. When the potter was satisfied that the correct temperature had been reached and maintained for sufficient time, the flue was sealed off and the kiln was allowed to cool down before opening.

Mesheck Sims unloading the kiln at the Cross Roads Pottery in the 1930's.

UNLOADING

The kiln was allowed to cool for several days before the job of unloading began. Any pots which were damaged and unfit for sale were thrown over the side of the kiln. These built into a mound of wasters around the kiln, which not only insulated it but provided excellent evidence for archaeologists, as they are virtually indestructible.

THE PRODUCTS

We have little evidence of what Dorset potters were producing until the middle of the seventeenth century, although documents tell us that the industry had been in existence for four hundred years before the 1640 Horton pottery. The peak of the industry was in the seventeenth century, when the potters supplied a vast range of wares ranging from ridge tiles to dainty saucers. Their pots were mainly connected with the storage, preparation and presentation of food and drink and the needs of the farm, dairy and brewhouse – both in the town and country. This emphasis was continued into the eighteenth century, although the range of wares slowly decreased.

Gradually the range of wares contracted even further. Only forms such pitchers (jugs), cream pans, sets of bushel pans and the famous costrel, known as the 'Dorset Owl' (named because its shape resembled an owl) survived. Potters were trying to keep up with the fashionable styles that were coming south from the industrial potteries of the Midlands and other areas. To compete with this factory production they introduced new products including ornamental flower pots, jardinieres, vases, wall pots, egg cups, casseroles, money boxes and ash trays.

A late nineteenth century money box incised with the words
'Joseph Shering, maker, Verwood, Dorset.'

The hawker, 'Pans' Brewer, selling pots by horse and wagon in the 1920's.

SELLING THE WARE

In medieval days pottery would have been transported over a relatively short distance by packhorse. As roads improved so the use of a horse and wagon became practical and evidence is enriched by nineteenth century records and verbal recollections.

The names of about thirty nineteenth and twentieth century hawkers are known. They were usually related to the potters, but were not makers themselves, and earned their living by travelling with a horse and wagon selling the pots. Some travelled as far afield as Devizes, Southampton, Lyme Regis and the Isle of Wight. But most of the pottery was sold locally, and their wares were packed in straw or heather and sold to farms, private houses and big estates, such as Longleat and Cranborne. Shops were regularly supplied, such as the Co-op in Ringwood, Timothy Whites in Bournemouth and Coles Hardware in Wimborne.

Colourful characters, with names like Sydney Bailey, 'Pans' or 'Brush' Brewer, Job King, Lotty Oxford, Jessie Sims, Walter (known as 'Bubbles') Sims, and Martin Sims, were well known local hawkers. 'Pans' Brewer was one of the last of the hawkers and continued his journeys into the 1930's, gaining his nick-name from crying 'pots, pans and pitchers!' when passing through a village. Clive Thorne, who use to drive 'Pans' Brewer round by van after he had retired his horse, recalled receiving instructions to 'whoa there!' and 'steady down!'. Brewer's horse-drawn itinerary was covered at a stately four miles an hour, and included Bridport, Dorchester, Salisbury, Sherborne, Tisbury, Wareham, Warminster, Wincanton and Yeovil.

Sydney Bailey, a familiar local hawker, always wore a bowler hat, whilst another, Job King, did conjuring tricks for children. and is reputed to have added to his income by regularly selling his cat for sixpence – who in due course returned home! Another hawker, Walter, or 'Bubbles' Sims, went hawking with his father and remembered staying at the Horton Inn for two pence, which included a clay pipe and an ounce of tobacco, bread and cheese washed down with ale, a rough bed for himself and stabling for his horse.

The railway brought its own advantages. Hawkers could put a load of pots onto a train, go off with their wagon well loaded, sell all their wares, reload from a distant station (maybe Southampton), and work

Display of Verwood pots for sale at Spicers shop, Dorchester, in the 1880s.

their way home again – thus doubling their potential income from a circular journey. Some hawkers were even said to visit another pottery and sell different wares on the way home.

Records dating to the late nineteenth century give some indication of the prices they were charging. A set of three large pans, (bushel, peck and half bushel) cost 3/6d (18p). Butter churns (known as a Dorset Plump) sold for 1/6d (7p) and cream pans for 7d (4p). It is said that the hawkers brought the pots at about half the retail price. thereby allowing some compensation for the inevitable breakages which occurred during transit.

By the 1940's the day of the hawker had ended. The roads which in the early days had enabled them to sell their wares further afield were now to hurry their decline. The car and lorry had taken over, and an ever-widening range of other types of pottery was increasingly available. The arrival of plastics was the final nail in the coffin. 'Pans' Brewer and 'Bubbles' Sims went into permanent retirement.

POOLE POTTERY AND ITS NEIGHBOURS

Dorset gradually became well-known nationally for its clays, particularly the ball clays dug in the Purbecks. Nearby Poole, as a trading centre, became the obvious site for the development of architectural potteries in the nineteenth century. Poole Pottery, undoubtedly this century's best known Dorset pottery, grew out of this historic background. As the arrival of the railways improved communications, prospectors from the Midlands and other areas began to look at the Poole area for opening new pottery works.

The Patent Architectural Pottery in Hamworthy was set up by local people and businessmen from Staffordshire in 1855. One of their technicians, James Walker, left to set up his own business on East Quay, but the business was not a success. In 1873 Jesse Carter, formerly an ironmonger and builders' merchant in Surrey, bought and enlarged this pottery. By taking his sons Charles and Owen into partnership in 1881 he started a family business whose connections were to last into the 1960's. Today it is one of Dorset's most thriving industries.

Jesse Carter bought another pottery in 1895, known as the Architectural Pottery Company. Here he began to produce glazed earthenware and terracotta, whilst the Hamworthy pottery (known as the White Works because it made white tiles) initially produced floor tiles before increasing its range to majolica and terracotta. He also owned deposits of red clay in Corfe Mullen.

In 1901 Jesse retired and his sons, Owen and Charles, formed a new company which they called Carter & Co. Owen began to develop decorative pottery. He was influenced by the work of William de Morgan, a close friend of William Morris, who had been buying blank tiles, bowls and dishes from the Architectural Pottery

Most of the Poole Pottery ware dating from 1926 was designed by Truda Carter. Here left to right: Ann Hatchard, Eileen Pragnell and Gertie Rivers are hand-painting traditional Poole Pottery.

since the 1870's. This decorated ware became the foundation on which this pottery made its name. The new style attracted many contemporary painters and designers, and in 1904, a young designer, James Radley Young, rejoined the pottery after an unsuccessful attempt at running his own business in Surrey. He was to make an important contribution to the decorations, styles and forms at this time. The firm now produced majolica and terracotta garden ware, including fountains, pergolas, balustrades and large pots decorated with interlaced bands and knots in Celtic style. Carter and Co. became one of the main suppliers of tiles and architectural decorations in Britain in the 1920's and 1930's. Pottery was also produced for the Omega workshops of the art critic Roger Fry. Amongst the throwers and designers employed by the pottery were the two sisters Lily and Gertie Gilham. Lily left to get married in 1923, but after joining in 1931 Gertie stayed on as one of the chief throwers till 1950.

Owen Carter specialised in researching and making lustre glazed pieces. He also made stoneware vases, bowls and jardinieres in simple thrown shapes, some with moulded relief decoration. His work was glazed in a great variety of colours. His later experiments produced unglazed bricks that were intended to be filled with perfumed oil, for which he designed a special miniature kiln. Owen

The 'Bull', designed by Harold and Phoebe Stabler in 1914.
Made at Poole Pottery from 1922.

Carter died when still young in 1919, but so established was the new decorative pottery business that although the production of architectural ceramics was still the main source of income, the painted ware had already made its mark.

Charles and his son Cyril Carter took over the running of the business. Charles introduced Cyril to the designer and silversmith, Harold Stabler (who with his wife Phoebe was later renowned for his figures and garden ware), who in turn introduced Cyril to John Adams, a technical potter and designer born in Staffordshire. In 1921 a subsidiary company, Carter, Stabler and Adams was formed to market its wares under the name of Poole Pottery. They received commissions from railways, department stores, banks, London Transport stations and swimming pools, as well as the Hoover factory and Lyons Corner House restaurants in London, the Cunard liners *Queen Mary* and *Queen Elizabeth* and for the 1951 Festival of Great Britain.

This new partnership revolutionised the pottery. John Adam's wife,

Racing yachts, probably designed by John Adams and modelled by
Harry Brown. Poole Pottery, 1937–1938.

A Poole Pottery plate called the 'Waterwitch', designed by Margaret
Holder in 1931 from a drawing by Arthur Bradbury.

Truda Carter, brought into the pottery a style that reflected the
Art-Deco movement. This in turn introduced a bright multi-coloured
free-hand painting which was applied to tableware, ornaments,
nursery ware, brooches, tiles and other forms. This stylised pottery
has been produced ever since and has given Poole Pottery its
distinctive character.

The pottery struggled to survive the Second World War. By the
time it was over, Harold Stabler was dead and John Adams in poor
health. However Cyril Carter, with the support of the new works
director, Roy Holland, encouraged massive investment that enabled
the pottery to once again flourish. A new team of designers sprung
up under the direction of Alfred Read and Ruth Pavely, Ann Read

Poole Pottery vase, designed by Truda Carter in about 1938.

Examples of the pots made by Guy Sydenham for Poole Pottery
in the 1970s.

and Guy Sydenham, who together did much to inspire the revival of
the pottery's reputation.

Guy Sydenham, who lived on Long Island and Green Island in
Poole Harbour, became well known for the production of his salt
glaze pots. In 1977 he left Poole Pottery to set up, with his son
Russel, a new enterprise called Quay Pottery. He now lives in
Portland and has set up a new workshop called Mermaid Studio,
whilst Russel runs the New Barn Pottery at Bradford Peverell, near
Dorchester.

The 1950's and 1960's saw many notable designs develop in the
hands of Robert Jefferson, Guy Sydenham and Tony Morris. Their
success attracted many talented painters and designers, who in turn
all helped put Poole Pottery well and truly on the map. Designs
such as 'Delphis', 'Aegean' and 'Atlantis' carried the pottery into the
1970's.

Both Cyril Carter and Roy Holland retired in 1964 and the family

A range of Poole Pottery tableware called 'New England'. The pattern was designed by Anita Harris in 1995 and introduced a new sponged technique of layered colours.

firm combined with Pilkington's Tiles of Manchester as part of the Thomas Tilling Group. Trevor Wight was employed as the new managing director and new products continued to flow into the 1990's, including the rapidly expanding table and gift range created by the Queensbury Hunt partnership, Robert Jefferson and Robert Welch. Barbara Adams designed stoneware sculpture, Tony Morris a series of cathedral and calendar plates and Elaine Williamson factory designs.

In 1992 Poole Pottery regained its independence. Its design director is now David Queensbury, and its ever-expanding and changing patterns and forms have won it an international market. Throughout its history, its diversity of products has been remarkable, ranging through earthenware majolica, tiles, lustre ware, domestic and ornamental ware, Art Deco and avant garde to traditional flower painting.

Three other Dorset potteries stand out as examples of the renaissance of the craft movement in the twentieth century: Sibley and Keysworth, both close to Wareham, and the Dorset Crown pottery, which is nearer to Poole. Their wares differ from Verwood as they produced decorative ware such as tea sets, coffee pots, jugs and bowls, rather than the more agricultural bushel pans, cream dishes and butter churns made in Verwood.

In *Unknown Dorset* (1927), Donald Maxwell records how near Wareham he stopped at a local pottery – the Sibley Pottery – 'a Peter Pan industrial venture, half hidden in pine trees and revealing not only industry but art'. Set on the edge of Egdon Heath, Sibley Pottery was established in 1920 by Rachel Bennett and two partners, Bertie Collin and Amy Krauss, who in 1932 moved to Corfe Castle to set up her own pottery.

The potters, who used the local ball clay, developed a variety of glazes ranging from dark greens and oranges to blacks, producing tea sets, jugs, bowls and the like. It was the black glaze that attracted

A black tea set ordered for a friend from the Sibley Pottery by
T.E. Lawrence (of Arabia) in about 1934.

The Keysworth Pottery, near Wareham, in about 1912.
From a catalogue produced by Lady Baker.

T. E. Lawrence (of Arabia), who whilst living at Cloud's Hill near Bovington visited the pottery and ordered two tea services, one for himself and another for a friend in the desert – the latter set even had its plate edges curved inwards to avoid sand getting into the food.

It is known that a total of four black tea sets were made. Lawrence had become a good friend of Thomas Hardy and his wife. After Hardy's death in 1928 his widow, Florence, ordered a similar set in memory of the happy occasions when they had had tea at Cloud's Hill and Hardy had admired Lawrence's black tea set. The fourth set appears to have been made for the use of friends staying at the cottage, so if any accidents occurred one set remained intact, and it can still be seen in Cloud's Hill today.

Rachel Bennett married Captain Warner in 1926, who in turn nursed it through years of economic uncertainty. The pottery survived, but Bertie Collin retired in 1929 due to ill health. This left

Jim Smith, who had joined the pottery earlier and remained a faithful mainstay until he died in 1939. The pottery ran three kilns known as Pa, Ma and Baby for their sizes, and also for the size of pots that could be fired in them. With Jim Smith's death the pottery seemed to quietly fade away, and on the outbreak of war the buildings were requisitioned by the army. In 1945 Branksome China leased the pottery for 14 years, and any large production of pottery at Sibley finally ceased in 1959.

Keysworth Pottery was started by Lady Amy Baker in 1910. Having already established a pottery at Burley in the New Forest she began looking for other premises and came across an old brickyard in Keysworth which seemed ideal for the production of her terracotta

A display of Keysworth Pottery presented by Wareham Town Council to the Duke of York (later George VI) on his marriage to Lady Elizabeth Bowes-Lyon in 1923.

ware. David Tolson was her manager and lived on the premises with his wife and children. Billy Clarke worked as an assistant to David Tolson for four years and can recall making jugs, lemon squeezers, vases, soap dishes, bowls, candlesticks and the like. His weekly wages started at 7/6d (37p), rising to 9/- (45p) when he left to work for the Sandford Pottery – by which time he was entrusted with throwing and glazing but not firing a kiln. Production ceased in the late 1930s and Lady Baker died in 1940.

Loggias, rose pergolas, garden steps and columns were also made at Keysworth. The columns were priced at 5/- (25p) and were from ten to twelve feet high. From Lady Baker's catalogue in about 1912.

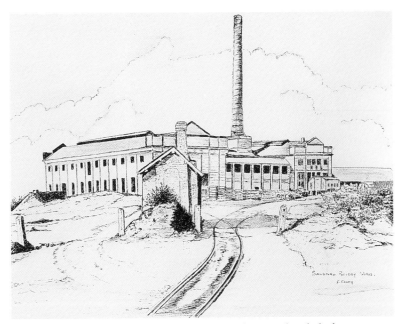

A drawing of Sandford Pottery by Fred Fancy shortly before
it was demolished in the 1970's.

The pottery at Sandford was established in 1860. The business was
taken over by the Shaw family in 1895 and they ran it until production ceased in 1966. George, Norman and Meg Speers worked for
the Shaws and George (age 86) recalls that potters were brought from
Staffordshire in an attempt to produce fine china. This was aban-
doned in favour of bricks and stoneware particularly chimney pots,
drainage pipes, garden edging and kitchen sinks, and at the height of
production over seventy people were employed at the factory. On
25th November 1979 the buildings were demolished.

Crown Dorset Art Pottery was established in Poole in 1905 by
Charles Collard, who set up his workshops and kilns in two adjacent
houses. The clay was dug locally at Lytchett Minster or Corfe
Mullen. The main thrower was Sam Main, whilst his brother Jim was
a decorator. The ware was decorated with a white slip, biscuit fired
for 24 hours and then decorated with glazes made to Charles
Collard's own recipes of blues, greens, browns and yellows, often

A small bowl with three handles in typical Dorset colours of greens, browns and creams. Incised into the red clay is 'Bournemouth' and 'Never say die, up man and try'. Crown Dorset ware probably made by Charles Collard, early twentieth century.

with sgraffito mottoes in the Dorset dialect under bright clear lead glazes, like contemporary Devon wares – which is where Collard originated. He was a popular employer and encouraged his teenage workers to attend Art School on day releases or evening classes, allowing them freedom of interpretation in the designs. He built up a healthy export market, on which he became reliant. So much so that when exports ceased during the First World War he was compelled to sell the business to George Paine in 1915, who five years later sold it on to the Dorset Art Pottery. It is known that containers were produced for the Wessex Pottery and Perfume Company, but it finally closed down in 1927.

The Purbeck Pottery was started in Westbourne, Bournemouth, in 1966 by a splinter group of potters and designers from Poole Pottery. Today they produce robust table stoneware for every day use, and the company is reputed to be the second biggest producer of stoneware in England. In 1990 it moved to Hamworthy, where it continues to flourish under the stewardship of one of the sons of its founders.

A group of Purbeck Pottery ware, some of it hand-painted, together with most of the lines currently manufactured by the pottery.

A twentieth century two-tone cup, saucer and plate from Branksome Pottery.

Ernest Baggaley, a manager at Poole Pottery, left in 1945 to open his own business as Branksome China. He leased facilities at the old derelict Sibley pottery, essentially for use as a sales outlet. Later the business moved to Fordingbridge in Hampshire, where it took over the old cinema and produced table ware in coloured English Porcelain. Ernest Baggaley died in 1987 and his wife and son continue running the business.

MODERN CERAMICS

With so much of Dorset's history rooted in ceramics, it is not surprising that the tradition lives on in the numerous potteries within the county. It is only possible in a book of this length to highlight the work of a very few, all of whom have continually worked in Dorset for a number of years, mainly using firing methods similar to the traditional potters of East Dorset.

Richard Batterham is probably the most celebrated living potter in Dorset. He went to Bryanston School and was taught by the legendary Don Potter, who also inspired Sir Terence Conran and David Queensbury. Bryanston was followed by some years spent in St Ives under the watchful eye of Bernard Leach, and he set up his own workshop near Blandford in the 1950s. He prepares his own clay and glazes, and fires an oil burning kiln. He does not invite publicity and his work carries no mark or signature, but he has shown that a small workshop can function economically. Not only does he sell extensively within the British Isles, but such is reputation abroad that his work can be seen in museums and private collections all over the world. He produces mainly functional ware, in a simple but distinctive style with luscious natural wood ash glazes, which are a joy to behold.

The Eeles family have a thriving family pottery business in Mosterton, West Dorset. David Eeles has been working as a potter for half a century, moving to Dorset in 1962. Together with his wife Patricia and sons Benjamin and Simon, he produces a wide range of dishes, platters, vases, bottles, and domestic ware with a skill which betrays David and Patricia's early training as painters. Their stoneware and porcelain is made at the pottery using such ingredients as granite, limestone, clay, basalt and sand. Most pots are fired in their large home-built wood-fired kiln, holding about 5000 pieces. It is good to see them continuing the Dorset tradition of family potting.

Above A two gallon jug made by David Eeles in iron clay slip, with a wax resist pattern and blue coloured glazes.
Opposite page A tall bottle in pale ash glaze by Richard Batterham.

Jonathan Garrett's display at Hare Lane pottery. Jonathan Garrett
is on the right.

Right in the heart of where the East Dorset Potting industry once flourished, Hare Lane Pottery sprung to life in 1986. Jonathan Garratt works on his own making frostproof terracotta pots by hand from local clays and fires them in a round, wood-burning kiln. The clay is brought by tractor from a local farm, and once weathered for a year is put into a 'blunger', liquidized with rainwater and sieved onto drying beds to dry to throwing consistency. The clay blocks are taken to the pugmill and 'pugged' twice with a little plastering sand. The pugmill is essentially a glorified mixer with steel blades on a rotating shaft inside a horizontal tube which extrudes required lengths of homogenous clay. This is then taken in to the workshop and weighed into balls of appropriate weight for throwing.

Throwing is done in batches. The finished ware is placed on boards to dry, over a stove in winter and outside in the summer. This can take six weeks for the biggest pots. Careful nursing of drying pots is vital to prevent warping and cracking. Once dry, the ware is taken to the kiln shed and placed round the kiln. Three days are needed for packing the kiln, which holds more than a ton of pots. It is round, seven feet across by seven feet high inside and has four fireboxes for wood, with a twenty five feet chimney. It comprises some twenty thousand bricks and took several months to build.

After packing, firing begins early the next day and continues for eighteen hours until 1120 degrees centigrade is reached, when stoking is stopped and the kiln is shut down. It cools for three days until the inside temperature has fallen to below 200 degrees. Then the door of loose bricks is removed and the pots are withdrawn. Wood ash is dusted off and the pots are placed in the yard outside. Jonathan also makes a selection of glazed table-ware, firing with wood to develop beautiful warm colours from lemon yellow to blood orange and mahogany. Other pots are glazed in green or blue and white. His wonderful outside display is reminiscent of the old potteries, which were traditionally surrounded by examples of their work.

Adrian Lewis-Evans began his training under Norah Braden at Camberwell Art College, setting up a pottery in Lytchett Matravers following the purchase of a disused brick works in 1958. He produces stoneware vases, jugs, mugs, tankards, Dorset 'Owl' cider

A copper red and blue alkaline flashed bottle
by Adrian Lewis-Evans.

flagons, table lamps, bonsai and wall hanging pots and terracotta garden ware glazes. He is known internationally and exports some of his Dorset 'Owls' and other work to America. For many years he taught ceramics at Bournemouth and Poole College of Art, and many Dorset-based potters owe their choice of profession to his guidance and teaching.

Matt-Hew Davies was inspired as a boy by the well-known potter Guy Sydenham. In the mid 1980s his parents bought Green Island in Poole Harbour, where Guy was then potting. Watching him work, Matt's future began to be shaped. Ar Bryanston School he enjoyed the teaching and encouragement of Don Potter, after which he studied Ceramics at Bournemouth and Poole College of Art & Design and West Surrey College. Matt now works on Green Island himself, following in Guy Sydenham's footsteps. He produces wonderfully large, tall, narrow-necked pots - like wine amphora – and

Hand-thrown stoneware by Matt Davies, wood-fired with ash slips.

A cut-sided jug in wood ash glaze over iron slip with
combed decoration made by Paul Green.

pots with narrow necks but more full-bellied. His great interest is
salt glaze, but he also uses other materials, including rhododendron
wood - which is thrown into the kiln and creates some amazing
effects. He uses various slips, made from local clays, which give an
entirely different texture to his pots.

Paul Green was encouraged by a teacher who had been heavily
influenced by the father of the British studio pottery movement –
Bernard Leach. He moved to Cerne Abbas in 1986 to set up Abbey
Pottery, producing functional pottery to suit both the table and oven.
He mixes his own glazes, such as tennoku, celadon and cobalt blue,

Three miniature one-twelfth scale 'blue dash' chargers in English Delftware by Carol Lodder. Hand-painted on tin glaze, depicting grapes and pomegranates, from a late seventeenth century design.

but favours the colour and surface glazes of wood ash. He also produces individual pieces, including some porcelain. There is gentle decorating on some of his pots, but the emphasis is very much on the form.

Carol Lodder runs her miniature pottery business from her home in North Dorset. She trained at Bournemouth Art College, where she was tutored by David Ballantyne and Peter Stoodley. An important influence has been Michael Cardew, who taught her how to dig her own clay, make her own glazes and how to fire a wood burning kiln. Her finger-nail size table and kitchen ware are much in demand by dolls' house collectors and owners. She produces reproduction hand-painted English Delftware, seventeenth and eighteenth century country ware, nineteenth century and present-day ware, including terracotta for the garden and Chinese and Japanese porcelain. Her hand-thrown 1/12th scale miniature pots are accurate in every detail, and are much sought after by enthusiasts and collectors.

FURTHER READING

Much information is taken from David Algar, Anthony Light and Penny Copland-Griffiths' *Verwood and District Potteries – A Dorset Industry* 2nd ed. (1987) published by The Verwood and District Potteries Trust, which was compiled from primary sources by interviews with those who in some way were connected with the industry.

Documentary evidence and photographs have been loaned from the Verwood & District Potteries Trust, which was set up in 1985 to promote interest in the history, development and manufacture of pottery within the East Dorset area, and to encourage the preservation of the East Dorset heathland, with particular reference to those areas that relate to the pottery industry. Inquiries should be sent to: The Secretary, Verwood & District Potteries Trust, Trowle House, Wingfield, Trowbridge, Wiltshire BA14 9LE.

Information on Poole Pottery was obtained during discussions with Guy Sydenham and from the following publications: Jennifer Hawkins *The Poole Potteries* (1980), Lesley Hayward's *Poole Pottery – Carter & Company and their Successors 1873–1995* (1995) and Jo McKowen's *Poole Pottery, the first hundred years* (1973).

Details on Dorset Crown Pottery were obtained from Carol and Chris Casmore's *Collard – The Honiton and Dorset Potter* (1982) and Martin Hammond's article in a newsletter of *The Verwood and District Potteries Trust. Newsletter.* 'Crown Dorset Art Pottery', No 25, December 1993.

Brian Berryman, present owner of the Sibley pottery, supplied much information, as did Jill Warner, daughter-in-law of Rachel Warner. Michael Warner's articles in *Dorset County Magazine*, 'Pots and people in the Sibley Pottery', 1990, and in *The Thomas Hardy Year Book, 1976*, 'Sibley Pottery' were also useful.

Billy Clarke, now in his 91st year, and who trained as a potter under Mr Tolson at Keysworth in the 1920's, gave a wonderful insight into Lady Amy Baker's pottery, as did a letter in the *Dorset County Chronicle* by Amy Baker on 15th February, 1910.

Information on Branksome pottery was supplied by Mrs Baggaley, widow of Ernest Baggaley. Mr Barnes, grandson of the founder of Purbeck Pottery, kindly supplied information on the development of the business.

Evidence on the earlier history of potting comes from articles by: Jo Draper, 'An 18th century kiln at Holt Common, Lyme Regis', *Proceedings of the Dorset Natural History and Archaeological Society* 104. (1982), Paul Spoerry with V. Hart, 'Documentary and Other Evidence for Medieval and Post-medieval Ceramic Production in Dorset' in the same journal 110. (1988), and JohnTerry, 'East Holme Pottery', also in the *Proceedings*, 109 (1987).

All the modern potters described have kindly supplied information on their potteries. Other publications and books quoted are: A.D. Mills, *Dorset Place-Names* (1986) and William Stevenson *A general view of the Agriculture of Dorset* (1815).

ACKNOWLEDGEMENTS

I am particularly grateful to Jo Draper, whose tremendous support and enthusiasm added so much to the enjoyment of writing this book; to my husband, Michael, who has never complained at proof-reading or being woken to discuss some aspect of its contents; and to my late friend and the last worker in the Verwood Potteries, Len Sims, who over twenty years provided so much information and help. My sincere thanks to David Algar and Tony Light, to whom I owe so much; and to Ian Waterfield, my companion in many hours of research and interviewing. I am also grateful to Leslie Hayward for his help, Christopher Chaplin for the maps; and would beg the forgiveness of anyone I might have inadvertently left out.

My thanks go to those who have given freely of their time over the years to tell me the story of their involvement in the industry, namely: the late Arthur Bailey, the late Margery Bailey, Richard Batterham, Maud Brewer, the late Drummer Brewer, the late Ken Brewer, Mr & Mrs Gordon Broomfield, the late Harold Churchill, Matt-Hew Davies, David Eeles, the late Harold Ferrett, Jonathan Garratt, Paul Green, Adrian Lewis-Evans, Cliff Lockyer, Ivor Lockyer, Carol Lodder, the late Gertie Sims, the late Clifford Sims and his brother and sister, the late George Sims, the late Walter Sims, Owen Sims, the late Donald Young, and the Zebedee family.

My final thanks are to the craftsmen potters and potteries for providing so many of the illustrations. All the photographs of Verwood and the East Dorset potteries are from my own collection or that of the Verwood & District Potteries Trust, but I would particularly like to thank the following: Julian Comrie for the photographs of Richard Batterham's work and the Keysworth Pottery: Dorset County Museum: pages 57, 64: Fred Fancy; page 61: Leslie Hayward; the front cover, pages 51, 52, 53, 54: Poole Pottery; page 55, 56: Purbeck Pottery; page 62; Jack and Olive Rogers; page 24.

The

DISCOVER DORSET

Series of Books

A series of paperback books providing informative illustrated
introductions to Dorset's history, culture and way of life.
The following titles have so far been published.

All the books about Dorset published by The Dovecote Press
are available in bookshops throughout the county,
or in case of difficulty direct from the publishers.
The Dovecote Press Ltd, Stanbridge,
Wimborne, Dorset BH21 4JD
Tel: 01258 840549.